The Best 50
MARINADES

Dona Z. Meilach

BRISTOL PUBLISHING ENTERPRISES
San Leandro, California

Printed in the United States of America.

ISBN: 1-55867-274-5

Cover design:	Frank J. Paredes
Cover photography:	John A. Benson
Food stylist:	Susan Devaty
Illustration:	Caryn Leschen

THE MAGIC OF MARINADES

A marinade is an easy-to-mix seasoned liquid in which foods are soaked.

Marinades make ordinary cooking extraordinary. They enhance the flavor of good foods, add interesting tastes to bland foods and break down and tenderize tough fibrous elements in meats, poultry and game. Marinades preserve many foods and introduce variety to everyday menus to help save you money.

Raw meats, fish, poultry, game, vegetables and fruits can all be marinated. The results will be spectacular appetizers, salads, entrées and desserts.

Marinated foods can be combined with other foods. Flavored vegetables will perk up soups. Marinated (often called macerated) fruits can be added to puddings, pies and cakes.

Some marinated foods are eaten raw and some are cooked. If cooked, they may be prepared by every method normally used: roasting, broiling, microwaving, frying and grilling.

The costs of using a marinade are minimal as is the effort involved. The last-minute cook may have to alter procedures slightly because marinades must be prepared ahead and foods soaked in them before preparing or serving. However, cooking time for marinated foods is often reduced by as much as one-third.

MARINADE BASICS

A marinade consists of just a few basic ingredients:

- an acid, such as vinegar, wine, lemon juice or beer. Acids break down fibers, tenderizing them and allowing flavors to enter. Acids also help retard bacterial growth and preserve foods.

- seasonings such as herbs or spices. Seasonings add delicious flavors. Salt (a mineral, not a spice) and sugar or honey have several functions: they impart flavor, heighten the flavors of other ingredients, preserve food and help retard bacterial growth. Use a minimal amount of salt in meat recipes as it tends to draw out juices. Salt is more important in fish marinades, as drawing out moisture makes fish flesh firmer and tastier. Remember that dried herbs, spices and seasonings have a limited shelf life; flavors deteriorate after 8 to 12 months.

- sometimes an oil, such as olive oil or vegetable oil. Oil adds moisture and smoothness, and in the case of olive oil, flavor. Oil helps to carry flavorings into the fibers. Remember, however, that vegetable oils have only a 3- or 4-month shelf life.

Ideally, a marinade should enhance the food, not overpower it. The recipes offered here are designed so that you can cook "by the book." But if you like to experiment, do so. You can select a basic marinade and, by changing the herbs and spices and the liquid base, completely alter the character of the food.

Before you begin, here are a few tricks of the trade.

- It is preferable to marinate foods in a glass, ceramic, enamel or stainless steel container, because acids react to cast iron, aluminum or copper, causing chemical changes, rust and bitter tastes. Marinating in plastic is not recommended when using the same plastic container repeatedly, because over time plastic can absorb oils and flavors that cannot easily be washed away. However, there are exceptions. Disposable plastics make marinating convenient and safe: you can put the marinade in a locking food storage bag with the food and place the bag in a low bowl, turning the bag occasionally so that all the pieces of food are covered with the marinade. When the food has been marinated, the bag is discarded.

- Always blend the marinade ingredients well. Stir them with a wooden spoon, shake them in a jar, or mix them in a blender container or food processor workbowl.
- Foods to be marinated for less than 1 hour may be left out at room temperature. For longer marinating times, store foods in the refrigerator in a covered dish or sealed bag so that strong seasonings won't reach other foods. ***Foods marinated for long periods at room temperature are subject to dangerous bacterial growth.***
- Always marinate fresh or completely thawed foods. Do not marinate frozen foods, as the thawed liquid will dilute the

marinade. Wipe foods dry with paper towels before marinating.

- Foods that have already been marinated may be frozen before they are cooked, if they have not been previously frozen.
- Marinating time varies by food. The tougher the meat, for example, the longer the marinating period — perhaps as long as 2 days. Delicate fish may require 1 hour or less to marinate.
- The marinade liquid may be prepared in advance and stored in a jar in the refrigerator overnight, or until ready to use to allow flavors to develop. Fresh herbs and spices require more time than dried ones. Use fresh ingredients for long marinades and dried herbs and spices for shorter periods.
- Usually the marinade is drained from the dish before the food is cooked. The marinade can be reserved for basting or for thickening juices used for sauces and gravies. ***Reserved marinades must be boiled for at least 3 minutes after meats, fish and poultry are removed from them, as they may be subject to dangerous bacterial growth. Marinades should not***

be kept and reused.

- Generally, because marinated foods are tenderized, cooking time may be reduced by as much as one-third. Use a meat thermometer for meats, poultry and fish.

- You can premix your favorite combinations of herbs and spices and have them handy for easy use. Instead of buying expensive flavored vinegars, you can make your own (see page 8).

- Most marinade recipes are mixed as liquids at room temperature. Those that are cooked should be cooled to room temperature or chilled before adding them to the food.

SUGGESTED SUBSTITUTES

garlic: use an equal amount of shallots or scallions
herbs: 1 tbs. fresh herbs = $1/_3$ tsp. dried
honey: 1 cup = 1 cup packed brown sugar or 1 cup white sugar
juniper berries: use an equal amount of red jelly or jam
mustard, prepared: use an equal amount of dry mustard mixed with water, wine, vinegar, lemon juice or milk to the consistency of

prepared mustard

oils: vegetable oils or olive oil or mixtures of ½ vegetable oil and ½ olive oil

onions: use an equal amount of chives, scallions or shallots

salt: use an equal amount of lemon or lime juice

shallots: use an equal amount of scallions

spices: about 1 tbs. fresh for ⅓ tsp. dried or ground (example: ginger)

stock: Japanese miso can be substituted as a liquid stock

Tabasco Sauce: Make your own hot pepper sauce by stirring together 1 tbs. cayenne pepper, 2 tbs. sesame or vegetable oil and ½ tsp. sesame seeds. When used in marinades, do not store marinade longer than 48 hours.

tarragon vinegar: white vinegar with a touch of crumbled tarragon leaves

vermouth, red: use an equal amount of red wine

vermouth, dry: use an equal amount of dry white wine, dry sherry or sake

vinegar: use an equal amount of any other acidic liquid, or make your own flavored vinegar using one of 2 methods:

1. Heat 1 pt. plain vinegar or red or white wine vinegar to boiling. Pour over 1 tbs. dried herbs or spices of your choice in a 1-pint sterilized bottle. Cool and seal. If fresh herbs are available, use 1 sprig for each pint of vinegar.

2. Add herbs and/or spices in the same proportion as with the previous method to cold vinegar. Steep for 4 weeks. Filter, rebottle in sterilized containers and keep it tightly corked.

Suggested combinations include vinegar with tarragon, dill, rosemary, basil, marjoram or oregano. A clove of minced garlic or 1 tbs. of minced onion may be added, if desired. If garlic is used, crush the clove and remove it after 24 hours.

wine: use an equal amount of vermouth, or mix water with another acidic liquid such as vinegar or lemon juice in equal parts.

yogurt: use an equal amount of sour cream, or low-fat or nonfat sour cream.

THE MAGIC OF MARINADES

APPETIZERS

Fruit appetizers are easy to make. Almost all fresh, frozen and drained canned fruits can be marinated in a compatible liqueur, brandy or wine for 1 to 2 hours before serving.

VEGETABLES

Marinated vegetables keep so well, they are still good the second day. Marinade ingredients should be mixed thoroughly before adding them to the vegetables. Then refrigerate all together in a marinade-safe container for at least 1 hour. Fibrous vegetables such as beans, peas, tomatoes, carrots, cucumbers, zucchini, artichokes, mushrooms, asparagus and broccoli are best for marinating. Vegetables may be marinated raw or cooked.

Drain and reserve marinated vegetable juices before serving. Then freeze or refrigerate the juices and use them in soups. The juices contain abundant minerals and vitamins and the flavor is mild because the vegetables have absorbed most of the vinegar.

STEAKS, ROASTS AND HAMBURGER

Most meats marinate well in 1 hour at room temperature and 6 hours in the refrigerator. Do not marinate meat longer than 1 hours at room temperature (about 70°) because of potential bacterial growth. The tougher and larger the cut of meat, the longer the marinating time. Very large cuts may require 24 to 48 hours. Roasts and other thick cuts should be pierced to the center with a skewer or knife blade so that the marinade can penetrate and tenderize all the way through. It is not necessary to completely cover large cuts of meat with marinade. They can be placed with the marinade in a locking food storage bag or other container and turned frequently so all surfaces eventually absorb the marinade.

Use ³⁄₄ to 1 cup liquid to marinate about 1 ¹⁄₂ to 2 pounds of steak, since the meat does not have to be immersed completely. Steak should be marinated for 1 hour at room temperature or 2 to 4 hours in the refrigerator, and turned once.

Double the amount of liquid for a 3- to 5-pound roast. The marinade should reach about ²⁄₃ up the height of the roast, so place roasts in a deep bowl to marinate. Pierce meat deeply with a skewer in 3 or 4 places to allow marinade to penetrate.

After marinating, drain off liquid and use it for basting or to make sauce or gravy. Be sure to boil reserved marinade for at least 3 minutes before using. Broil or grill steaks and hamburgers, or bake hamburgers, allowing about 30 minutes baking time at 350°.

LAMB, VEAL AND PORK

The recipes for lamb, veal and pork may be baked, broiled or grilled. When you decide on a basic marinade, select the method of cooking from any one of the other recipes suggesting heat and time. Allow about ½ cup marinade for each pound of lamb, veal or pork.

POULTRY ENTRÉES

Many of the poultry recipes are designed to add color to the meat to make it attractive and appetizing.

Poultry should be well thawed and patted dry before marinating. Remove the skin if you choose. Pierce parts with a fork so the marinade flavors can penetrate the meat and tenderize it. Figure approximately ½ cup marinade per pound of chicken, or ¾ cup to 1 cup for a small chicken or the equivalent of 2 whole chicken breasts. Marinate chicken in marinade-safe containers in 1 or 2 layers and turn the chicken parts so the skin side is down once or twice during the marinating time, usually a minimum of 2 hours.

FISH AND SHELLFISH ENTRÉES

When you unwrap fish at home, do not rinse it under running water; instead, fill a pan with a solution of 1 qt. water and 1 tbs. lemon juice, rinse the fish in that and pat dry.

Be careful not to overmarinate fish. If the marinade does not cover the fish, either turn the fish over once during the marinating time or baste the fish with the marinade.

The greatest danger in preparing fish is overcooking. Uncooked fish is translucent; the second it becomes opaque, it is done. Test by flaking the thickest part with a fork or toothpick to check the color and texture. If a recipe calls for 10 minutes of cooking time, check it at 5 minutes and watch it carefully.

Generally, fish experts suggest a ratio of 10 minutes baking, broiling or grilling time to each inch of thickness. Measure the thickest part of the fish. A whole salmon that measures 4 inches thick will cook for 40 minutes. A 1½-inch-thick halibut steak requires approximately 15 minutes total or 7½ minutes per side.

KABOBS

Treatment of meat and poultry is essentially the same for all kabobs: Trim away excess fat and bones, cut meat into chunks about 1 to 2 inches square and marinate for several hours (about 2 hours if poultry) or overnight in the refrigerator. Thread meat onto skewers with or without vegetables and fruits, and then grill or broil. The kabob must be turned once or twice while broiling so all sides are cooked. Because many vegetables cook more quickly than meats, they must be watched carefully and brushed with marinade frequently during cooking. Vegetables and fruits can be cooked on separate skewers and served with the cooked meat cubes.

Generally 2 cups of liquid marinade will cover about 1 pound of meat cubes.

Some additional kabob tips:

- Presoak wooden skewers to prevent burning.
- Prevent ingredients from slipping off skewers by placing a large cube of bread brushed with oil at the pointed end.
- Vegetables that require longer cooking, such as onions, potatoes and zucchini, should be parboiled or placed on separate skewers. Begin to cook them before cooking meat or chicken.
- Always preheat the broiler; oil the pan or grill to prevent sticking.
- Keep slippery foods, such as raw oysters or chicken livers, under control by wrapping them in bacon or other meat. Intersperse soft foods, such as fish, with harder foods, such as zucchini, to give them all a firmer hold.
- Select ingredients for color and texture; combine crunchy with soft and smooth. Use complementary flavors: sweet and sour, smoky and nutty, zesty and mild.

THE MAGIC OF MARINADES

MINTED MELON ON SKEWERS

MARINADE
1/4 cup crème de menthe
1/4 cup lime juice
1/4 cup white wine
1 tsp. poppy seeds

1 cup cantaloupe balls or cubes

1 cup watermelon balls or triangles

1 cup honeydew balls or wedges

1 cup Persian or Crenshaw melon cubes or balls or other seasonal melon pieces

mint leaves for garnish, optional

Mix marinade ingredients and pour over fruit pieces in a bowl. Refrigerate, covered, for 3 hours. Drain. Thread melon pieces on short wooden skewers and pierce skewer tips into 1/2 of a watermelon shell placed upside down on a platter. Add mint leaves or other garnish in season. Makes about 6 servings.

PLUM AND BACON APPETIZERS

MARINADE
1 cup soy sauce
1/4 cup brown sugar, packed
3 tbs. wine vinegar
3 tbs. dry sherry
2 cloves garlic, minced

12 fresh Italian prune plums
3 oz. sharp cheddar cheese, cut into twelve 1/4-inch cubes
12 slices bacon

Slit 1 side of each plum only enough to remove pit and leave plum whole. Mix marinade ingredients in a medium saucepan. Add plums and heat to boiling. Reduce heat and simmer for 2 minutes. Marinate in the refrigerator, covered, for 4 hours.

Just before serving, drain plums. Place 1 cheese cube in each plum, wrap 1 bacon strip around each plum and secure with a pre-soaked wooden pick. Place plums on a wire rack over a baking pan to catch bacon fat. Broil 4 inches from heat, turning once, until bacon is crisp, about 4 minutes each side. Makes 12.

MARINATED CARROT SLICES OR STICKS

MARINADE
1/4 cup olive oil
2 tbs. wine vinegar
2 cloves garlic, minced
1 tsp. dried oregano
1/2 tsp. salt
1/2 tsp. pepper

8–10 large carrots
1/4 cup water

Peel carrots and cut into 1/2-inch slices or 1/2-inch-long match-sticks. Steam or microwave with water until crisp-tender. Drain. Place in a bowl with marinade ingredients and mix well. Marinate, covered, for at least 12 hours. Drain and serve on an appetizer platter. Makes 8 to 10 servings.

INDONESIAN SATÉS

MARINADE
1/4 cup chili seasoning mix
1/4 cup water
1/3 cup vegetable oil
1/4 cup lemon juice

---

2 1/2 lb. chicken breasts, skinned, boned and cut
into 1- to 1 1/2-inch cubes

Combine chili seasoning mix with water, oil and lemon juice.
Mix well and pour over chicken. Stir gently, cover and marinate in
the refrigerator for 4 hours. Remove chicken from marinade and
arrange on small wooden skewers that have been soaked in water.
Broil or grill for 4 minutes on each side, brushing with marinade.
Serve with *Peanut Sauce,* page 20. Makes 8 to 10 servings.

NOTE: Pork, lamb, beef or veal can be substituted for chicken.

PEANUT SAUCE

This sauce pairs well with Indonesian Sates, *page 19.*

1 tsp. chili seasoning mix
3/4 cup water
1 tbs. lemon juice
1/4 cup chunky peanut butter
1 tbs. chopped green onion for garnish

In a small saucepan, combine chili seasoning mix, water, lemon juice and peanut butter. Bring to a boil, stirring constantly, and cook until thickened. Garnish with green onion.

PEACH-FLAVORED GLAZED HAM CUBES

MARINADE
1 tbs. soy sauce
3 tbs. peach-flavored brandy or
liqueur
2 tsp. lemon juice

1 cup cubed cooked ham, in ³/₄-inch cubes

Mix marinade ingredients and stir into ham cubes until they are completely covered. Marinate for 1 hour. Drain. Heat under the broiler for about 3 to 4 minutes, turning with a spoon so all sides are glazed. Makes 4 to 6 servings.

LOMILOMI SALMON IN CHERRY TOMATOES

MARINADE
1 cup lime juice
1 large onion, minced
1 1/2 tsp. white pepper
1/4 tsp. sugar
1/4 tsp. hot pepper sauce

1 1/2 lb. salted salmon, cut into 1/4-inch cubes
3 pt. large cherry tomatoes, hollowed out
green onions or parsley for garnish

Place salmon cubes in marinade mixture. Refrigerate, covered, stirring occasionally, for 6 hours or overnight. Stuff salmon mixture into hollowed-out cherry tomatoes for individual appetizer servings. Garnish with green onions or parsley. Makes 12 to 14 servings.
NOTE: This is the Hawaiian version of marinated raw salmon.

SHRIMP IN MARINADE

MARINADE
1 1/4 cups vegetable oil
1/2 cup white wine vinegar
2 tsp. celery seed
1 tsp. salt
1 dash hot pepper sauce

2 lb. cooked, peeled, deveined shrimp
1 cup chopped green onions

Alternate layers of shrimp and green onions in a flat glass dish. Mix marinade and pour over shrimp. Cover and store in the refrigerator for 12 hours. Stir gently. Serve in a cocktail dish on shredded lettuce or directly from dish with cocktail picks. Makes 4 to 6 servings.

AVOCADO SALAD

MARINADE
1/2 cup vegetable oil
3 tbs. wine vinegar
3 tbs. lemon juice
1/2 tsp. sugar
1/8 tsp. salt
1/8 tsp. pepper

2 medium-sized ripe avocados
1/2 Bermuda onion, sliced
    paper-thin

1 orange, peeled and sectioned
shredded lettuce

    Peel avocados and cut into cubes. Place in a bowl with onion slices. Mix marinade and pour over vegetables. Cover and refrigerate for several hours, stirring occasionally. Just before serving, add orange pieces to salad and toss lightly. Serve on a bed of shredded lettuce. Makes 4 servings.

MUSTARD-HERB TOMATOES

MARINADE

¼ cup olive oil or vegetable oil	¼ cup chopped fresh parsley
1 tbs. tarragon vinegar	2 tsp. Dijon-style mustard
1 tbs. red wine vinegar	1 tsp. salt
1 clove garlic, crushed	1 tsp. sugar
	¼ tsp. pepper

3 large tomatoes, sliced

Cut tomatoes into ½-inch slices and restack slices to look like whole tomatoes in a serving dish. Mix marinade ingredients together until well blended and pour over tomatoes. Cover and refrigerate for 2 hours. Let stand at room temperature for 20 minutes before serving. Makes 5 to 6 servings.

FRENCH-CUT STRING BEANS WITH BACON AND WINE

MARINADE
½ cup cider vinegar
½ cup dry white wine
⅓ cup vegetable oil
½ cup sugar

1 lb. fresh or frozen string beans, cut French-style
6 slices bacon
1 medium onion, cut into narrow wedges
1 tsp. Dijon-style mustard
salt and pepper to taste

Prepare beans and cook in lightly salted water until just tender. Drain and place beans in a bowl. Cut bacon crosswise into strips about ⅛-inch wide. Fry in a skillet over moderate heat, stirring frequently, until light brown. Remove bacon from pan. Pour off bacon drippings, leaving just enough to sauté onion wedges. Stir until onion is tender, about 2 to 3 minutes.

Mix marinade ingredients and add to onion in pan. Slowly bring liquid to a boil, scraping bottom of skillet with a wooden spoon. Simmer for 3 minutes. Stir in mustard until well blended. Pour liquid over string beans. Add bacon, salt and pepper. Marinate in the refrigerator overnight. Serve in deep salad bowls. Makes 4 servings.

CARROTS IN SWEET PICKLE BRINE

MARINADE
1 1/2 cups sweet pickle brine, left over
from jar pickles
2 sprigs fresh parsley
1 thin slice fresh lemon

1–2 bunches baby carrots, 3–4 inches long, scrubbed but
unpeeled, or 1/2 lb. packaged baby carrots

Heat pickle brine, parsley and lemon to boiling. Add carrots and simmer for about 5 minutes until carrots are crisp-tender. Cool. Store in the refrigerator in a covered glass container for 4 to 6 hours, until thoroughly chilled. Makes 3 to 4 servings.

NOTE: These pickled carrots make a good addition to an appetizer platter. The next time you finish a jar of sweet pickles, save the brine to make this treat.

CUCUMBERS IN DILLED SOUR CREAM

MARINADE	
1 part vinegar and 1 part water, enough to cover cucumbers 1 tbs. sugar salt and pepper to taste	2 cups sour cream 2 tbs. lemon juice 2 tbs. tarragon vinegar ½ tsp. fresh dill 2 green onions, finely chopped

3 cucumbers, pared and thinly sliced
1 yellow onion, thinly sliced

Mix vinegar, water, sugar, salt and pepper for a preparatory marinade. Pour over cucumbers and sliced onions and refrigerate for 2 hours. Drain thoroughly. Mix remaining ingredients together and gently stir in drained cucumbers and sliced yellow onion. Chill until ready to serve. This dish can be prepared early in the day. Makes 6 servings.

LETTUCE, SPINACH AND ORANGE SALAD

MARINADE

3 tbs. vegetable oil
2 tbs. vinegar
2 tbs. corn syrup
1/2 tsp. seasoned salt

1/4 tsp. celery seed
1/4 tsp. dill seed
1/8 tsp. pepper

1 medium head iceberg or romaine lettuce
2 cups spinach leaves
2 tangerines or oranges, peeled, sectioned and cut in half
1/2 cup sliced onion, separated into rings

Tear lettuce and spinach leaves into bite-sized pieces. Mix marinade, pour over fruit and onion rings in a small bowl and marinate for 30 minutes. Just before serving, pour mixture over greens and toss. Makes 4 servings.

NOTE: For a luncheon salad, add one 15 oz. can of tuna, or 2 cups diced cooked chicken to tangerines and onions before marinating.

MINTED ZUCCHINI

MARINADE
1/2 cup vinegar
2 tbs. lemon juice
1 clove garlic, finely chopped
1 tbs. grated onion
1 tbs. chopped fresh mint or 1/4 tsp.
mint extract

2 medium zucchini, thinly sliced
1–2 tbs. vegetable oil

Sauté zucchini in oil, turning often until lightly browned. Transfer from skillet to a glass bowl. Cool. Mix marinade and add to zucchini. Chill for at least 1 hour. Makes 4 servings.

PICKLED RED ONIONS

MARINADE-PICKLING SOLUTION

2 cloves garlic, sliced
10 peppercorns
1/4 tsp. dried oregano

1/2 tsp. salt
3/4 cup vinegar (or enough to
cover onion in a 1-pint jar)

1 large red onion (about 1/2 lb.), thinly sliced

Place onion in a jar with garlic, pepper, oregano and salt. Add vinegar to cover. Cover jar and store in a cool place for 2 to 3 days before using. Makes 2 to 4 servings.

TERIYAKI MARINADE FOR BEEF

MARINADE

2 tbs. vegetable oil
2 tbs. sugar
2 tbs. sherry or dry white
   wine
1 tbs. soy sauce
1/2 cup beef stock (canned or
   made from bouillon cube)

1 clove garlic, pressed
1/8-inch piece fresh ginger,
   minced, or 4 tsp. ground
   ginger
salt and pepper to taste

2–3 lb. steak or hamburger

Marinate meat in the refrigerator for 4 to 6 hours or overnight. Drain meat and cook, using the method of your choice (see page 10). Makes 4 to 6 servings.

FAT-FREE WINE MARINADE FOR BEEF

MARINADE

¾ cup tarragon vinegar, wine vinegar or wine
1 medium onion, minced
½ cup chopped fresh parsley
1 ½ tsp. minced garlic
½ tsp. dried thyme or ground cumin
1 bay leaf, crushed
3 drops hot pepper sauce, or 1 dash dried red pepper flakes

2–3 lb. steak or hamburgers

Combine all ingredients. Marinate meat in the refrigerator for 2 to 4 hours. Drain meat and cook, using the method of your choice (see page 10). Makes 4 to 6 servings.

PORTERHOUSE STEAK
WITH ZESTY WINE MARINADE

MARINADE	
½ cup red Burgundy wine, or ⅓ cup bottled steak sauce 3 tbs. lemon juice 2 tbs. vegetable oil	1½ tsp. sugar ½ tsp. seasoning salt ¼ tsp. pepper

1 porterhouse steak, about 1½ inches thick, about 4 lb.

Combine marinade ingredients and pour over steak. Marinate for 4 hours in the refrigerator, turning meat occasionally. Drain and broil or grill. Makes 8 to 10 servings.

FLANK STEAK WITH ROSÉ WINE

MARINADE
3/4 cup rosé wine
1/4 cup vegetable oil
1 large clove garlic, crushed
1/2 tsp. salt
1 tsp. pepper

1 flank steak, about 2 lb.

Mix marinade and pour over meat. Turn meat to coat and place in the refrigerator, covered, for 3 to 4 hours. Drain and broil or grill. Thinly slice meat diagonally across the grain to serve. Boil remaining marinade for at least 3 minutes and use as sauce. Makes 4 to 5 servings.

KOREAN-STYLE BARBECUED BEEF

MARINADE

⅓ cup vegetable oil	3 cloves garlic, minced
⅓ cup soy sauce	2 tbs. toasted sesame seeds*
¼ cup sugar	1 dash hot pepper sauce
¼ cup minced green onions	½ tsp. salt

1½ lb. boneless beef round, sirloin tip or chuck steak,
cut into serving-sized pieces

Mix marinade ingredients and pour over beef. Marinate for 4 to 6 hours or overnight in the refrigerator. Drain marinade and grill meat. Heat marinade for sauce. Makes 3 to 4 servings.

*Toast sesame seeds in a 350° oven for 10 minutes, stirring frequently to prevent burning, or over medium heat in a dry skillet, stirring until browned.

STEAK ORIENTALE WITH ITALIAN DRESSING

MARINADE
1 cup prepared Italian salad dressing
1/4 cup soy sauce
2 tbs. brown sugar, packed

2–2 1/2 lb. steak of your choice, about 1–1 1/2 inches thick
1 green bell pepper, cut into chunks
1 onion, sliced

Mix marinade and add steak. Cover and marinate in the refrigerator for 4 hours or overnight, turning occasionally. Broil and brush with marinade. Broil green pepper and onion during last 10 minutes. Makes 4 to 6 servings.

FRENCH HOT DOGS

MARINADE

1 cup water
3 tbs. lemon juice
1 envelope (1-cup serving)
dry onion soup mix

1 envelope (1-cup serving) dry
tomato soup mix
1/2 tsp. dry mustard

8 beef frankfurters, scored
diagonally
1 tbs. flour

8 French bread rolls
1/4 cup grated Parmesan cheese

Prepare marinade and heat in a skillet, stirring constantly, until mixture boils. Remove from heat and add frankfurters. Let stand, covered, for 15 to 20 minutes. Remove frankfurters from marinade. Broil or grill 4 inches from heat for 7 to 10 minutes, turning frequently. While frankfurters cook, stir flour into marinade, reheat to boiling and stir until thick. Serve in French rolls, spoon marinade over frankfurters and sprinkle with cheese. Makes 8 servings.

MALAYSIAN HAMBURGERS

MARINADE
4 fresh mild chiles, seeded
1 dried red chile, broken into pieces
2 small onions, minced
1/2 tsp. minced fresh ginger
1/4 cup lemon juice
1 tbs. brown sugar
1 pinch saffron or turmeric
1 1/2 cups coconut milk
1/4 tsp. salt

1–2 lb. lean ground beef or chopped sirloin,
shaped as small meat loaves or flattened hamburgers

With a mortar and pestle, crush fresh and dried chiles. Mix into a paste with onions, ginger and lemon juice. Or add chiles, onions (quartered) and ginger root with lemon juice to a food processor workbowl and process until blended into a paste. Add sugar, saffron or turmeric, salt and coconut milk. Blend. Pour over meat and marinate in the refrigerator for 4 hours, turning meat frequently.

Drain. Bake in a 350° oven for ½ hour, or broil or grill. Boil remaining marinade for at least 3 minutes and use as sauce. Makes 4 to 8 servings.

MINT MARINADE FOR LAMB

MARINADE
$^1/_2$ cup water
1 tbs. cider vinegar
1 cup orange or clover honey
$^1/_3$ cup minced fresh mint, or $^1/_4$ cup
dried mint flakes

3–4 lb. lamb, any cut

Bring water and vinegar to a boil. Add honey and stir until dissolved. Remove from heat and stir in mint. Cool. Marinate for 3 to 4 hours in the refrigerator. Use to marinate any lamb cuts for broiling or barbecuing. Makes about 1$^3/_4$ cups, or enough for 8 to 10 servings.

FAT-FREE SPICE MARINADE FOR LAMB

MARINADE

1 cup wine vinegar
1 onion, chopped
8 whole cloves
2 sprigs fresh mint, or 1 tsp. dried
2 cloves garlic, crushed

4 sprigs fresh parsley, or 1 tsp. dried
1/8 tsp. dried thyme
1/8 tsp. dried tarragon
1 tsp. grated lemon zest
1/2 tsp. salt

1 lb. lamb, any cut

Mix all marinade ingredients and pour over lamb. Marinate for 3 to 4 hours in the refrigerator. Drain marinade and cook as desired. Makes 1 cup, for 1 or 2 servings of lamb chops or other lamb cuts.

LAMB CHOPS L'ORANGE

MARINADE

½ cup orange juice, or
   ¼ cup frozen orange juice
   concentrate, thawed
3 tbs. soy sauce

2 tsp. sugar
1 tsp. minced garlic
1 tsp. ground ginger
⅛ tsp. pepper

6 shoulder lamb chops, ¾-inch thick
2 oranges, cut into 6 wedges each
1–2 tbs. cornstarch

Arrange chops in a flat glass baking dish. Combine marinade ingredients, pour over chops, cover and refrigerate for 2 hours. Cover and bake with marinade at 350° for 1 hour, or until tender. Transfer chops to a serving plate and garnish with orange wedges. Skim fat from drippings; thicken drippings with 1 tbs. cornstarch per cup of juice. Spoon over meat and oranges. Makes 6 servings.

MEXICAN-STYLE BARBECUED VEAL CHOPS

MARINADE

$1/2$ cup cider vinegar	$1/2$ tsp. dried thyme
$1/4$ cup vegetable oil	$1/2$ tsp. ground cumin
$1/4$ cup ketchup	$1/2$ tsp. chili powder
$1/2$ cup minced onion	$1/4$ tsp. cayenne pepper
1 clove garlic, minced	$1 1/2$ tsp. salt

6 veal chops, $1 1/2$ inches thick, rinsed and dried

Combine marinade ingredients and add chops. Marinate in the refrigerator for 6 hours. Drain chops and broil 5 inches from heat for 15 to 20 minutes, or until brown. Baste with marinade during cooking. Makes 6 servings.

LEMON MARINADE FOR VEAL

MARINADE

3/4 cup wine vinegar
3 tbs. lemon juice
1 medium onion, minced
1 clove garlic, crushed
1 bay leaf, crumbled

1/4 cup chopped fresh parsley
1/8 tsp. dried thyme
1/8 tsp. dried tarragon
2 tsp. salt
1/2 tsp. pepper

2 lb. veal, any cut

Mix marinade ingredients and marinate veal in the refrigerator for a minimum of 4 hours. Drain and cook as desired. Makes about 1 cup marinade.

SPICE SEASONING MIX FOR PORK

SEASONING MIX

2 tbs. crumbled bay leaves	2 tbs. dried thyme
2 tbs. ground cloves	2 tbs. dried basil
2 tbs. mace	2 tbs. cinnamon
2 tbs. nutmeg	2 tbs. dried savory or parsley
2 tbs. paprika	5 tbs. white pepper

If you cook pork frequently, you may wish to prepare this special seasoning mix to add to the other marinade ingredients. The spice mix can be used with any combination of acid and oil in place of, or in addition to, those spices suggested in recipes for pork. The mix can also be used for pork roasts, pork chops, barbecued ribs, ham slices and patés, whether or not you are marinating them.

For any spices not already ground or crushed, you can use a spice grinder or electric blender. Mix ingredients and store in an airtight jar on the spice shelf.

CURRIED MARINADE FOR SPARERIBS

MARINADE
1/4 cup soy sauce
3 tbs. lemon juice
2 tbs. sherry
1 tsp. curry powder
2 cloves garlic, minced
1 1/2 tsp. instant tea dissolved in 1 1/2
cups water, or 1 1/2 cups very strong tea
1 tbs. *Spice Seasoning Mix for Pork*,
page 47
1/4 tsp. hot pepper sauce

4 lb. lean pork ribs
1 tbs. prepared mustard mixed with 1 tbs. honey

Strip membrane from back of pork ribs. If ribs are fatty, drop them in boiling water for about 5 minutes before marinating. Remove from water and wipe dry with paper towels. Place ribs in a shallow pan.

Combine marinade ingredients and pour over ribs. Cover and marinate in the refrigerator for at least 2 hours or overnight, turning so both sides soak in the liquid. Drain and reserve marinade to use for basting. For a final glaze, mix a little mustard with honey and brush on ribs.

To roast: Place ribs on racks in shallow pans and roast at 350° for 1¼ hours.

To grill: Place on grill 3 inches from low heat. Cook for about 1¼ hours, turning every 15 minutes. Makes 4 servings.

PORK BLADE STEAKS IN BEER

MARINADE
1 cup beer
1 cup bottled barbecue sauce
1/2 cup chopped onion
1 tsp. *Spice Seasoning Mix for Pork,*
page 47
1/8 tsp. minced garlic

4–6 pork blade steaks, cut 1/2–3/4 inches thick

Combine marinade ingredients. Marinate steaks in mixture in the refrigerator, covered, for about 4 hours, turning steaks several times. Remove steaks from marinade and grill over medium heat for 20 minutes on one side. Brush with marinade and grill other side until done, about 10 minutes on second side for a 1/2-inch steak, about 15 minutes for a 3/4-inch steak. Makes 4 to 6 servings.

BARBECUED HAM STEAKS

MARINADE
4 cups dry sherry
1/2 cup melted margarine or butter
4 tsp. ground cloves
4 tsp. paprika
1/2 cup brown sugar, packed
1/2 tsp. dry mustard
8 cloves garlic, finely chopped

6 ham steaks, about 1-inch thick

Combine marinade ingredients. Marinate ham steaks in mixture for 3 hours in the refrigerator, turning once. Broil or grill. Turn frequently and baste with marinade. Makes 6 servings.

POLYNESIAN MARINADE FOR CHICKEN

MARINADE
1/4 cup honey
1/4 cup fresh orange juice
2 tbs. fresh lemon juice
1/4 cup soy sauce
6 kumquats, finely chopped, or 2 tbs.
grated lemon zest
2 tbs. grated orange zest
1/2 tsp. ground ginger
1/4 tsp. pepper

1–2 chickens

Blend marinade ingredients well in a blender container.
Marinate chicken in the refrigerator for a minimum of 2 hours.
Drain chicken and cook as desired. Makes 1 1/2 cups for 1 to 2
chickens.

FAT-FREE LEMON MARINADE FOR CHICKEN

MARINADE

¾ cup wine vinegar
3 tbs. lemon juice
1 medium onion, minced
1 clove garlic, crushed
¼ cup chopped fresh parsley

1 bay leaf
⅛ tsp. dried thyme
⅛ tsp. dried tarragon
2 tsp. salt
½ tsp. pepper

1 small chicken, or 2 chicken breasts

Mix marinade and pour over chicken. Let stand, covered, for at least 2 hours in the refrigerator. Drain chicken and cook as desired. Makes ¾ cup for 1 chicken.

NOTE: For even less fat, remove skin and any visible fat from chicken before marinating.

JAM-BOREE BAKED CHICKEN

MARINADE I – RED

8 oz. prepared red salad
   dressing (such as Russian)
1/2 cup red or purple preserves
   or jelly (strawberry, grape,
   plum or a combination)
1 envelope dry onion soup
   mix

MARINADE II – GREEN

8 oz. prepared green salad
   dressing (such as Green
   Goddess)
1/2 cup light-colored preserves
   or jam (apricot, pineapple or
   peach)
1 envelope dry onion soup
   mix

1–2 chickens, cut into pieces

Mix marinade ingredients in a small bowl. Lay chicken pieces in a flat pan in a single layer and spread with marinade. Cover and refrigerate for 3 hours. Bake with marinade at 350° for 45 minutes to 1 hour. Makes 4 to 6 servings.

BAKED HONEY CHICKEN

MARINADE
1/4 cup soy sauce
1/2 cup ketchup
1/4 cup fresh lemon juice
1/4 cup honey or brown sugar, packed

2 frying chickens, halved or cut into pieces
cold water
1 tbs. cornstarch
hot cooked rice

Arrange chicken in a single layer in a flat dish and pour marinade over. Refrigerate for several hours or overnight. Cover with foil and bake for 1 hour at 325°. Remove foil, baste with sauce and bake uncovered for 10 to 15 minutes, or until tender and browned. To thicken sauce, mix a little cold water with cornstarch and stir into sauce. Serve over rice. Makes 4 to 6 servings.

BAKED TERIYAKI-WHISKEY CHICKEN

MARINADE
2/3 cup vegetable oil
2/3 cup soy sauce
2/3 cup bourbon
1 tsp. minced garlic
1/2 tsp. pepper

1 large frying chicken

Cut chicken into serving pieces, place in a single layer in a pan, and pour marinade mixture over each piece. Refrigerate for 4 hours or overnight. Bake in marinade, covered, in a 350° oven for 45 minutes, or until chicken is well done. Turn pieces frequently and baste with sauce. Uncover and continue baking until brown, about 10 minutes. Makes 4 servings.

CALIFORNIA BARBECUED CHICKEN

MARINADE
$1/2$ cup sherry
$1/3$ cup honey
2 tbs. lime juice
2 tsp. cinnamon
$1/2$ tsp. curry powder
$1/2$ tsp. minced garlic

2–3 lb. frying chicken, cut into pieces or quartered

Combine marinade ingredients and pour over chicken. Cover and refrigerate for 4 hours. Broil or grill 6 inches from heat until tender. Baste often with remaining marinade. Chicken will brown quickly, so watch it closely. Makes 4 servings.

TANDOORI CHICKEN BREASTS

MARINADE
1 cup plain yogurt
juice of 1 lime
2 green chile peppers, chopped
2 cloves garlic, minced
1 tsp. minced fresh ginger
1 1/2 tsp. ground coriander

4 chicken breasts, quartered and skinned
1/4 cup margarine, melted

Slash chicken diagonally with shallow cuts. Blend 1/2 of the yogurt with remaining ingredients. When well blended, add to remaining yogurt and stir to blend. Brush onto cut side of chicken and marinate for 8 hours or overnight. Remove chicken from marinade and broil or grill for 30 to 40 minutes. Coat with melted margarine before cooking. Brush with marinade while cooking and turn once. Makes 6 to 8 servings.

BANGKOK CURRIED CHICKEN AND FRUIT SALAD

MARINADE
$^1/_2$ cup mayonnaise
1 tbs. lime or lemon juice
2 tbs. curry powder
salt to taste

2 cups diced cooked chicken
1 cup shredded coconut
1 cup blanched golden raisins
1 cup chopped peanuts

1 cup sliced bananas
1 cup diced apples
1 cup diced celery
1 cup chutney

Mix marinade and add to all other ingredients. Toss lightly and marinate in the refrigerator overnight. Makes 12 to 15 servings.

NOTE: This recipe can be doubled for an elegant addition to a buffet supper for a crowd.

TERIYAKI TURKEY

MARINADE
1 1/2 cups soy sauce
1/2 cup lemon juice
1/4 tsp. ground ginger
2 cloves garlic, minced
1/4 cup minced fresh parsley

1 turkey hindquarter

Place turkey in a shallow dish. Mix marinade and pour over turkey. Turn to coat well. Cover and marinate in the refrigerator for several hours or overnight. Drain. Grill until tender and browned, 1 1/2 to 2 hours. Turn and baste with marinade as necessary to prevent burning. When turkey feels tender when pressed, cut into the thigh joint. If no red juices run, turkey is done. Slice across thigh and lengthwise on drumstick to serve. Makes 3 to 4 servings.

BARBECUED GARLIC SHRIMP

MARINADE

1 cup white wine	1/2 tsp. salt
1 tbs. chili sauce	1/2 tsp. pepper
1 lime or lemon, sliced	1/2 tsp. paprika
2 cloves garlic, sliced	1 dash dried oregano

1 lb. large raw shrimp

To prepare shrimp, cut heads off with a very sharp knife; slice down the back and remove black vein by rinsing shrimp under cold running water. Leave shells and tails on.

Mix marinade ingredients and marinate shrimp for 1 hour or more. Remove from marinade and broil or grill, turning and basting often. Or, bake in a 300° oven for about 30 minutes, basting often. Makes 4 servings.

BAKED SALMON WITH SWEET MUSTARD MARINADE

MARINADE
1/4 cup light brown sugar, packed
warm water
2 tbs. Dijon-style mustard
1/4 cup fresh dill or tarragon,
or 2 tbs. dried
3 tbs. olive oil

4–6 salmon fillets
lemon slices
1 purple onion ring
3–4 string beans or zucchini slices

Place sugar in a bowl. Sprinkle with just enough warm water to soften and begin to dissolve sugar. Add mustard and dill and stir together, adding oil as you stir. Place salmon fillets skin-side down in a glass baking dish. Spread marinade over fish and turn fish over a few times to coat. Leave in dish skin-side up. Cover and refrigerate for 2 to 4 hours.

Heat oven to 350°. Remove fish from marinade and place on aluminum foil in a baking dish. Place lemon slices, onion ring and string beans on each fillet and bake uncovered for 15 to 25 minutes, or until fish flakes easily with a fork. With a wide spatula, remove fish from pan and place on a serving dish. Makes 4 to 6 servings.

NOTE: This is a delicious combination for salmon, but it works as well on chicken.

TERIYAKI MARINADE FOR FISH

MARINADE
6 tbs. soy sauce
6 tbs. water or white wine
2 cloves garlic, crushed
1/4 cup fresh lime juice

whole fish, fish fillets, fish steaks or shellfish

Mix soy sauce, water or wine and garlic. Add fish or shellfish and marinate for 2 to 3 hours in the refrigerator. Drain. Bake or broil fish according to directions on page 13. Use lime juice to baste fish while cooking. Makes 3/4 cup marinade.

HAWAIIAN MARINADE FOR FISH

MARINADE
1 cup pineapple juice
1/4 cup vegetable oil
1 envelope (1 1/2 oz.) dry spaghetti
sauce mix, or 1/2 cup prepared
spaghetti sauce without meat

fish fillets

Combine marinade ingredients and marinate fish fillets for 1 to 2 hours in the refrigerator. Drain marinade and use for basting. Bake or broil fish according to directions on page 13. Makes 1 1/2 cups marinade.

TUNA FISH-PINEAPPLE TOSS

MARINADE

¼ cup vegetable oil
3 tbs. tarragon vinegar
3 tbs. juice from canned
  pineapple

½ tsp. ground cloves
1 tbs. crème de menthe or
  fresh mint leaves, or 1 tsp.
  mint extract

1 can (13½ oz.) water-packed
  tuna fish
1 can (4 oz.) pineapple chunks
  in natural syrup

lettuce
fresh mint leaves and tomatoes
  for garnish

Drain tuna fish. Mix marinade and pour over tuna; stir. Cover and refrigerate for 4 to 6 hours. Remove from marinade with a slotted spoon. Drain pineapple chunks and gently mix into tuna. Serve on a bed of lettuce garnished with mint leaves, tomatoes and other vegetables in season. Makes 2 to 3 servings.

FISH AND SHELLFISH

NORTHWEST FISH STEAK GRILL

MARINADE

1 cup dry vermouth
3/4 cup vegetable oil
1/3 cup lemon juice
2 tbs. chopped chives
2 tsp. salt
1 clove garlic, finely chopped

1/4 tsp. dried marjoram
1/4 tsp. pepper
1/4 tsp. dried thyme
1/8 tsp. dried sage
1/8 tsp. hot pepper sauce

2 lb. salmon, halibut or other fish steaks, fresh or frozen

Thaw steaks if frozen. Cut into 6 portions and place in a single layer in a shallow baking dish. Combine marinade ingredients and pour over fish. Refrigerate, covered, for 4 hours, turning occasionally. Remove fish and reserve sauce for basting. Place fish on a well-greased hinged wire grill. Cook about 4 inches from moderately hot coals for 8 minutes. Baste, turn and cook for 7 to 10 minutes, or until fish flakes easily when tested with a fork. Makes 6 servings.

APPLE-FLAVORED CHICKEN KABOBS

MARINADE
$^1/_2$ cup beer
$^1/_2$ cup juice from fresh pineapple
2 tbs. vegetable oil
1 tbs. soy sauce
1 clove garlic, crushed

4 whole chicken breasts, halved and skinned
salt and pepper to taste
8 mushrooms
8 small white onions
8 cherry tomatoes
2 oranges, peeled and quartered
2 pineapple slices, quartered

Bone chicken breasts and cut each half-breast into 4 pieces. Sprinkle chicken with salt and pepper. Alternate chicken pieces with mushrooms, onions, cherry tomatoes, orange quarters and pineapple quarters to make 8 skewers. Place skewers in a shallow pan. Combine marinade ingredients and spoon over kabobs. Let stand for 1 hour. Drain and broil or grill 6 inches from heat for 15 minutes on each side. Brush with marinade every 5 minutes. Makes 8 servings.

PERSIAN CHICKEN KABOBS

MARINADE
1/4 cup vegetable oil
1/4 cup tarragon wine vinegar
1/2 tsp. dried mint leaves
1/4 tsp. dried rosemary
1 clove garlic, crushed
1/4 tsp. hot pepper sauce

4 chicken breasts, halved, skinned and boned, cut into 2-inch pieces
1 tsp. salt
4 medium tomatoes, quartered

16 small white onions
6 green bell peppers, seeded and cut into skewer pieces
16 small to medium mushroom caps

Sprinkle chicken with ½ tsp. salt. Mix marinade and pour over chicken in a flat dish. Refrigerate for at least 2 hours or overnight, turning once or twice. Drain and reserve liquid for basting.

Thread chicken pieces on skewers, alternating with tomatoes, onions, green peppers and mushroom caps. Brush with marinade. Sprinkle with remaining ½ tsp. salt. Broil or grill about 6 inches from heat for 30 minutes, or until chicken is done, turning and basting while cooking. Serve with rice pilaf or cooked rice.

LAMB KABOBS WITH BEER-PINEAPPLE MARINADE

MARINADE
1/2 cup beer
1/2 cup juice from fresh pineapple
2 tbs. vegetable oil
1 tbs. soy sauce
1 clove garlic, crushed

1 1/2 lb. lamb shoulder or leg,
  cut into 1 1/2-inch cubes
1 large green bell pepper
2 large tomatoes

2 small onions
8 cubes fresh pineapple, 2
  inches each

Mix marinade ingredients. Add lamb and refrigerate, covered, overnight. Seed and cut pepper into 2-inch cubes. Quarter tomatoes. Peel and quarter onions. Drain marinade and reserve. Alternate lamb, vegetables and pineapple pieces on skewers. Brush with marinade while broiling. Makes 4 servings.

BASIC FRUIT JUICE MARINADE

MARINADE
1/2 cup orange juice or other fruit juice
grated zest and juice of 1/2 lemon
1/4 cup maple or corn syrup
1 vanilla bean, or 6 coriander seeds,
crushed
1/4 cup brandy or liqueur, optional

---

fresh fruit, peeled and sliced, diced or quartered

Thoroughly mix all marinade ingredients and pour juice over fruit. Marinate in the refrigerator, covered, for 4 hours, occasionally stirring gently. Let stand at room temperature for about 20 minutes before serving.

SPICED ORANGE SLICES

MARINADE
1/2 cup sugar
1 cup Burgundy wine or claret
1 vanilla bean
1 stick cinnamon
12 whole cloves
1 lemon, thinly sliced

6 oranges, peeled and sliced about 1/4-inch thick
1/2 cup raisins, optional
whipped cream

In a saucepan, mix marinade ingredients together. Bring to a boil and simmer for 15 minutes. Remove lemon and spices and pour sauce over orange slices and raisins. Marinate, refrigerated, for 24 hours. Baste occasionally. Serve with whipped cream. Makes 4 to 6 servings.

MARINATED FRUIT DESSERTS

HONEY AND WINE BERRY MARINADE

MARINADE
1/2 cup orange honey
1/2 cup sweet sherry or orange juice

2 cups berries (strawberries, raspberries, blueberries or other)

Combine honey with sherry. Pour over prepared fruit and marinate in the refrigerator for at least 1 hour. Serve chilled. Makes 4 servings.

INDEX